C000000893

Cats

Illustrated by Jenny MacKendrick

The History Press

First published 2016

The History Press
The Mill, Brimscombe Port
Stroud, Gloucestershire, GL5 2QG
www.thehistorypress.co.uk

Illustrations © Jenny MacKendrick, 2016

The right of Jenny MacKendrick to be identified as the Illustrator
of this work has been asserted in accordance with the
Copyright, Designs and Patents Act 1988.

All rights reserved. No part of this book may be reprinted
or reproduced or utilised in any form or by any electronic,
mechanical or other means, now known or hereafter invented,
including photocopying and recording, or in any information
storage or retrieval system, without the permission in writing
from the Publishers.

British Library Cataloguing in Publication Data.
A catalogue record for this book is available from the
British Library.

ISBN 978 0 7509 6755 6

Design by The History Press
Printed in China

Cats ...

think they are gods,

and come in all different colours,

and all different sizes.

Some are fluffy,

some are not.

Some are beautiful,

some are not.

But they are all inscrutable,

insufferable,

and prone to attacks of madness.

Cats need ...

warmth,

entertainment,

freedom

and attention.

They need a safe place to hide

and a base for attack.

They need to be loved,

no, adored,

and stroked ...

but not too much.

Cats are ...

always asleep

but always awake.

They are creatures of habit,

immune to discipline,

territorial,

forgetful,

hard to please,

persistent,

scrupulously clean

(most of the time)

and loving

(when it suits them).

Cats like ...

cardboard boxes

(however uncomfortable)

and paper bags.

They like to be in charge,

of the big

and the small.

They like to make their presence felt

or to disappear for days.

Cats like people who don't like them,

or at least they seem to ...

Cats don't like ...

competition,

getting wet

or being disturbed.

They don't like change,

worming tablets

or aerosols.

They hate to be over-fussed

but they hate to be ignored.

They don't like dogs

unless it's *their* dog.

Cats have ...

twitchy ears,

sensitive noses,

sharp claws,

nine lives,

six senses

no. 23,796

and a million ways to wash themselves.

They have conveniently short memories,

cunning plans

and clever tricks,

impeccable timing

and perfect balance ...

usually.

Cats will ...

sleep anywhere,

however uncomfortable,

just to prove a point.

They will get under your nose

and under your feet

and into your hair,

but are only affectionate on their own terms.

Cats will bring you presents

(whether you want them or not).

They will never let you down

and never let you forget them

even after they are gone.

About the Illustrator

Jenny MacKendrick studied drawing and applied arts at the University of the West of England. She now works as an artist and illustrator from her studio in Bristol, which she shares with Shona, her large and hairy Hungarian Wirehaired Vizsla, who is often to be found hiding under the desk.

Also in this Series
Border Terriers
Labradors
Pugs
Springer Spaniels

www.thehistorypress.co.uk